The Smallest Horses

Story by Jenny Giles

Illustrations by Sharyn Madder

On Saturday, Clare's dad said,
"Let's go to the dog show today.
I would like to see the farm dogs."

"So would I," said Clare's mom.

But Clare had been
to dog shows before,
and she didn't want to go.
She liked looking at horses, not dogs.
"Do I have to come?" she asked.
"Couldn't I go and play
at Abby's house?"

3

But when Abby
heard about the dog show,
she wanted to go to it.

"Oh well," said Clare.
"If Abby comes, it will be more fun."

When they got to the show,
they watched the dogs walking around
the show ring with their owners.

There were lots of dogs.
The show went on and on
for a long time.

After a while,
Clare and Abby got tired
of watching the dogs.

"Let's go for a walk," said Mom.

Dad said,
"I can meet you in the parking lot
in about half an hour."

As Mom and the girls
walked past a big building,
they saw a sign.

"A pet show!" said Clare.
"Can we go and see it?"

Inside the building,
they saw some dogs with puppies
and some cats with kittens.

There were birds in cages,
and fish in tanks.

The girls walked around
looking at everything.

Then they saw a lot of people
over in the far corner.
"I wonder what they are looking at,"
said Clare. "Let's go and see."

"I'm sorry, Clare," said Mom,
looking at her watch.
"Dad will be waiting for us."

"But it's the only thing
we haven't seen!" said Clare.
"Please, Mom!"

"All right," said Mom.
"But you will have to hurry."

At first,
the girls couldn't see anything.
Everyone was in their way.

"Come on," said Mom.
"We have to go."

But just then,
some people moved away.

"Oh!" cried Clare and Abby.
"Oh!"

Clare and Abby stood very still.
There, in front of them,
were two tiny horses.

The horses were not even
as tall as the girls!
The woman who owned them
let Clare and Abby pat them.

"You can't ride these little horses,"
she said.
"They are just kept as pets."

"These little horses are so cute!"
said Clare.

"And we nearly didn't see them,"
said Abby.